# We Are Not Alone

When Paul Cookson is alone he likes to write his own poems, read other people's poems, listen to loud music, watch videos, eat sweets and play his guitar badly. Sometimes all at the same time. He lives in Retford with his wife and son.

David Parkins has illustrated numerous books, ranging from maths textbooks to *The Beano*. His picture books have been shortlisted for the Smarties Book Prize and the Kurt Maschler Award; and commended twice in the National Art Library Illustration Awards. He lives in Lincoln with his wife, three children and six cats.

# We Are Not Alone

Poems chosen by Paul Cookson

Illustrated by David Parkins

MACMILLAN
CHILDREN'S BOOKS

Dedicated to the staff and pupils
of the Firs Junior School, Birmingham

First published 1999
by Macmillan Children's Books
a division of Macmillan Publishers Ltd
25 Eccleston Place, London SW1W 9NF
Basingstoke and Oxford
www.macmillan.co.uk

Associated companies throughout the world

ISBN 0 330 37521 0

135798642

A CIP catalogue record for this book is available from the British Library.

Printed by Mackays of Chatham plc, Chatham, Kent.

# Contents

# Aliens are Sending Me Messages

Aliens are sending me messages
I'm getting instructions from outer space

> *Stop washing your hands*
> *Your neck*
> *Your face*

Aliens are sending me messages
I'm getting instructions from outer space

> *Eat more chocolate*
> *More ice cream*
> *More cakes*

Oh, I like the instructions I'm getting
These messages from outer space

> But Mum says if I obey them
> My teeth will rot
> And I'll smell.

> And Dad's convinced
> It's a crafty plot
> To end the human race.

**STARTING WITH ME!**

But, of course, it's not.
Those aliens seem like a sensible lot
And deserve nothing but praise.

And I'll tell you what:
As long as they keep sending me messages
(Instructions from outer space)
I'll continue guzzling chocolate
And never ever wash my face!

Bernard Young

Eat chocolate

Don't wash

# The Terrible Path

While playing at the woodland's edge
I saw a child one day,
She was standing near a foaming brook
And a sign, half-rotted away.

There was something strange about her clothes.
They were from another age.
I might have seen them in a book
Upon a mildewed page.

She looked pale and frightened.
Her voice was thick with dread.
She spoke through lips rimmed with green
And this is what she said:

*'I saw a signpost with no name,
I was surprised and had to stare,
It pointed to a broken gate
And a path that led nowhere.*

*'The path had run to seed and I
Walked as in a dream.
It entered a silent oak wood
And crossed a silent stream.*

*'And in a tree a silent bird
Mouthed a silent song.
I wanted to turn back again
But something had gone wrong.*

'The path would not let me go;
It had claimed me for its own,
It led me through a dark wood
Where all was overgrown.

'I followed it until the leaves
Had fallen from the trees,
I followed it until the frost
Drugged the autumn's bees.

'I followed it until the spring
Dissolved the winter snow,
And whichever way the path turned
I was obliged to go.

'The years passed like shooting stars,
They melted and were gone,
But the path itself seemed endless,
It twisted and went on.

I followed it and thought aloud,
"I'll be found, wait and see."
Yet in my heart I knew by then
The world had forgotten me.'

Frightened, I turned homeward,
But then stopped and had to stare.
I too saw that signpost with no name,
And the path that led nowhere.

Brian Patten

# Kraken

One thousand years he's lurked now
beneath Atlantic waves;
his tentacles coil gently
round careless sailors' graves.
He sinks and whirlpools open
that swallow man or beast;
he swims – a tidal wave begins
engulfing west and east.

He's heavier than a hurricane,
as tall as redwood trees;
his arms can grip the biggest ship
that sails the seven seas.
His eyeball is like Jupiter
and when he blows out spray
it covers earth and moon and sun
for three weeks and a day.

So should you ever hoist your sails
near transatlantic deeps,
though all seems calm, remember
the restless Kraken sleeps.
Don't set your sails too boldly
in transatlantic deeps;
*though all is calm, remember,*
*the Kraken merely sleeps ...*

Judith Nicholls

# Yeti

A trail
Of footprints

Leading nowhere.

A trick
Of the light.

Blurred photographs.

In certain high valleys,
Biding our time,
They wait . . .

**Kevin McCann**

# Ready Salted

Nothing else happened
That day.

Nothing much, anyway.

I got up, went to school,
Did the usual stuff.

Came home, watched telly,
Did the usual stuff.

Nothing else happened
That day,

Nothing much, anyway,

But the eyeball in the crisps
Was enough.

Ian McMillan

# I'm Home (Safe and Sound)

To meet with a Bigfoot would *scare me to death!*
But I've had a recurring dream
That, one day, I'll find myself trapped and alone –
And no one will hear when I scream!

So I'm hurrying home, through the woods, late at night –
Watching for eyes in the dark;
Noting each scrunch of the ground underfoot;
Scared that I'll hear something bark.

It's great to reach home, place my key in the lock,
Enter my house, bolt the door;
But the lights won't turn on,
Though I try every switch –
So the power must be off – and, what's more,
There's no one at home
And each room is pitch black;
All is silent and chill, there's no heat;
So I make for the lounge
And sink down on a chair,
Which has two hairy arms . . .

And large feet . . .

*YAAAHHHH!*

Trevor Harvey

# Figure and Ground

It was after
Whatever happened –
Whatever happened?
I can't remember.
But it was after,
And I was walking
Along a street I think that once I must have known.
I was alone
But then he came towards me,
A young boy,
Intent upon the bouncing of a ball.
Nearer he came, and nearer,
Bounce and skip,
And then he passed right through me
And I turned,
And watched him bouncing, skipping up the road
And did not know
I was the ghost, the ghost who passed through him,
But thought
He was the ghost, a ghost who passed through me.
And I was most afraid.

                                        Pam Gidney

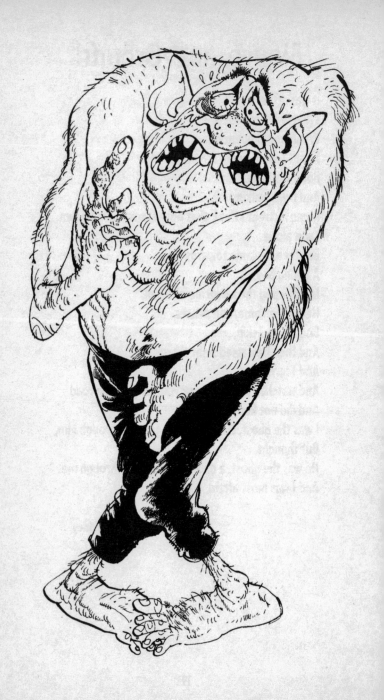

# We All Have To Go

The sound drew nearer;
a wheezy, hoarse breathing
as if some heavy weight
were being dragged along.
There was a smell of burnt bones.
A horny, hairy finger edged
round the trickling, slimy wall.
Then a large warty nose,
topped by bloodshot watery eyes,
slowly emerged from the gloom.
The eyes widened, glowing
to a bright red.
Its pace quickened and soon
it towered above us.
The huge slavering mouth opened –
'Any of you lot know where
the toilet is?'

                              John C. Desmond

# Greengrocer

I went into the greengrocer's:
the vegetables and the fruit
were all piled neatly in their boxes
and a large watermelon lay in the corner.

I couldn't see the greengrocer.
The shop smelt ripe and drowsy. I put
three bananas in a paper bag. It was
so still and silent I felt watched.
The mushrooms looked like knee bones.
The watermelon lay contented in the corner.

What had happened to the greengrocer?
I took some carrots. I stuffed
plastic bags with spinach,
with the long green teeth of okra,
with courgettes like tiny truncheons.
The watermelon lay big-bellied in the corner.

There was no sign of the greengrocer.
I called out, I waited, then I left
money by the till and went towards the door.
The enormous watermelon in the corner
snored.

Dave Calder

# We Are Not Alone

When the floorboards creak and hinges squeak
When the TV's off but seems to speak
When the moon is full and you hear a shriek
We are not alone.

When the spiders gather beneath your bed
When they colonise the garden shed
When they spin their webs right above your head
We are not alone.

When the lights are out and there's no one home
When you're by yourself and you're on your own
When the radiators bubble and groan
We are not alone.

When the shadows lengthen round your wall
When you hear deep breathing in the hall
When you think there's no one there at all
We are not alone.

When the branches tap on your window pane
When the finger twigs scritch scratch again
When something's changed but it looks the same
We are not alone.

When the wallpaper is full of eyes
When the toys in the dark all change in size
When anything's a monster in disguise
We are not alone.

You'd better watch out whatever you do
There's something out there looking at you
When you think you are on your own
We are not
We are not
We are not alone.

**Paul Cookson**

# Two Witches Discuss
# Good Grooming

'How do you keep your teeth so green
Whilst mine remain quite white?
Although I rub them vigorously
With cold slime every night.

'Your eyes are such a lovely shade
Of bloodshot, streaked with puce.
I prod mine daily with a stick
But it isn't any use.

'I envy so, the spots and boils
That brighten your complexion.
Even rat spit on my face
Left no trace of infection.

'I've even failed to have bad breath
After eating sewage raw,
Yet your halitosis
Can strip paint from a door.'

*'My dear, there is no secret,*
*Now I don't mean to brag.*
*What you see is nature's work,*
*I'm just a natural hag.'*

John Coldwell

# Pillow Monsters

When all is quiet under the duvet
You will hear
The pillow monsters feeding,
Munching dreams
And gobbling snores like truffles.
Nightmares give them indigestion!
Territorial beasts –
Put two together
And a fight is sure to break out.
Then the feathers fly!
A word of warning –
Never feed them after 6 a.m.

Sue Cowling

# The Visitor

It was late last night I'm certain
wasn't it?
That I saw my bedroom curtain
twitch and flutter
felt a chill, heard him mutter
'Hello lad, I'm back.'

Uncle Jack
dead since this night last year
wasn't it?
A pickled onion in his beer
stopped his breath, a sudden death
that took us sadly by surprise.

But there he was, those eyes
one grey, one blue
one through
which the light could pass
the other, glass.

He drifted down, swam about
didn't he?
In his brown suit, flat cap, stout
boots and tie
I saw him remove his eye
didn't I?

'It's not a dream
this,' he said, 'don't scream,
I'll not come back, I shan't return,'
then I felt the ice-cold burn
of his glass eye on my skin.
Saw his ghastly ghostly grin,
'Don't worry, don't get in a stew,
just thought I'd keep an eye on you.'

When I woke up today
I saw the blue eye not the grey.
But when I picked it up to go
it drained away like melting snow.
Didn't it?

**David Harmer**

# Who Knows About UFOs?

If UFOs are Unidentified Flying Objects –
Whose job is it to identify them?

And, once identified, does a UFO become an IFO?

And, if a UFO can no longer fly –
Perhaps due to a technical problem –
Does it become a UO?

And, if I threw my slipper in the air –
And nobody knew what it was –
Would it too be a UFO?

I think I'll file these questions under
Useless Factual Observations.

James Carter

# Beware

Across the moon
Like veins of black
The dead tree's
Branches show.
Against the bark
Shadowed by cowl
She stands with
Eyes aglow.
'Tis her night tonight my friends.
Keep windows locked and barred.
'Tis Hallowe'en,
'Tis Hallowe'en.
'Neath moon and cloud
In moaning wind
She moves
And
Aaaaaaahhhhhh . . . . . . . . . .

Redvers Brandling

# The Invisible Man

The invisible man is a joker
Who wears an invisible grin
And the usual kind of visible clothes
Which cover up most of him,

But there's nothing above his collar
Or at the end of his sleeves,
And his laughter is like the invisible wind
Which rustles the visible leaves.

When the visible storm clouds gather
He strides through the visible rain
In a special invisible see-through cloak
Then invisibly back again.

But he wears a thick, visible overcoat
To go out when it visibly snows
And the usual visible footprints
Get left wherever he goes.

In the visible heat-haze of summer
And the glare of the visible sun,
He undoes his visible buttons
With invisible fingers and thumb,

Takes off his visible jacket,
Loosens his visible tie,
Then snaps his visible braces
As he winks an invisible eye.

Last thing in his visible nightgown
Tucked up in his visible bed
He rests on a visible pillow
His weary invisible head

And ponders by visible moonlight
What invisibility means
Then drifts into silent invisible sleep
Full of wonderful visible dreams.

John Mole

# I'm Right Here

I'm the dream
You didn't want to have
The nightmare driving you mad.

I'm the monster
In the bushes in the park
The footsteps ringing after dark.

I'm the vampire
Flapping round your room
The darkness, shadow and gloom.

I'm the Nasty
The Horrid and Spite
The hairy scary feeling in the night.

I'm the reeking, speaking, stomach tweaking
Staircase creaking whilst you're sleeping
Creeping so your heart is leaping
Thing.

I'll sing
My werewolf song
Bring along my friend King Kong.

My bones
Will rattle your ears
My moans and groans will stir your fears.

What's that?
Well they are mine
Those tingling fingers down your spine.

Don't scream
Don't make a sound
I'm right here, don't turn around.

David Harmer

# Crop Circle Hair

One morning, my brother,
when combing his hair,
shrieked to discovered
a crop circle there.
'Aliens have landed,'
he moaned, 'in the night.'
But the rest of the family
just laughed at the sight.
'It's ruined my hairstyle,'
he grumbled. 'Oh, well,
I'll soon get it out
with my super strong gel.'
Next morning, he woke
with a pain in the head
and there, wrecked in flames
and untidying the bed
was a small, alien spaceship.
My brother yelled 'Yikes.'
It had gone to its doom
on his supergelled spikes.
His hair, slightly singed,
was still smoking. Surprised
he watched as the spaceship
and crew vaporised.
But our parents, who gave him
no time to explain,
assumed he'd been playing
with matches again
and grounded him, now

he sits sulking, aggrieved
at being a victim
who nobody believed
and he plans, though the aliens
and spaceship are gone,
to sleep with his windows
shut from now on.

Marian Swinger

# Granny's Door

In Granny's hallway was a door.
A locked door. It was always locked.
'What's in there?' I often asked.

And Granny would shiver slightly.
She would glance over her shoulder
and say softly (at the edge of

her breath):
'I can't tell you.
I *really* can't tell you.'

When Granny died and Mum and Dad
were clearing her trivia and her treasures
I found a key of tarnished brass

hidden in an old, cracked pot
at the back of the cupboard
in her bedroom.

When Mum and Dad weren't looking
I tried the key in the door
and it opened. A musty smell

greeted me like an ill brother
and led me down the steps
into the damp darkness.

And what did I find?
I can't tell you.
I *really* can't tell you.

Roger Stevens

# Watching

What if I told you
The stars in the sky
Were not really stars at all

But eyes

Winking and blinking
And spying on you
Watching your every move

Try and imagine it

Now try to fall asleep
On a clear night
If you can.

Andrea Shavick

# The Boy Who Was Nearly Swallowed Up by the Cupboard Under the Stairs

In those long, unfillable days after Christmas,
when parents lie in and days slow down
to cloud-passing pace,
a boy came home from the football field
muddied and red-faced, hot and wearing
too many clothes, having misjudged the temperature.

Into the kitchen to grab a swig of drink
and a doorstep cheese sandwich –
the studs of his football boots
clacking and slipping on the tiled floor
and leaving a trail of mud and grass
that would look perfect for
a floor-cleaner advert set-design.

'Get that ball off the kitchen table
and get those boots off right now – outside!'
He kind of expected this yelled double demand,
so it came as no surprise.
In fact he was already making
his way to the back door.

Football in hand and in stocking soles,
he sockboarded across the kitchen floor
spreading the muck like an abstract in the Tate.

Into the hall and open the latch
on the cupboard under the stairs
(tight as a muscle man's bathroom tap!)
– and there's this little sound,
not quite a cat-call, not quite a dog-yawn,
not quite an animal and certainly not a baby.

Dark in there, the only light-coloured thing
is the hoover and even it's partly covered with raincoats.
He tries to throw the football in, any-old-where.
But it falls back out, in fact is thrown back out.
So he tries placing it.
Placing it on top of the pile of shoes,
but it doesn't take hold, just rolls off.

And then, sounding like an orchestra careering into chaos,
there's a shout from the kitchen, something falls
on the landing making a great crashing noise,
without warning the dog jumps up on his back
almost pushing him into the cupboard
so he shoves the ball in between the fleeces, overcoats
and sports jackets. Shoves it in hard as he can
with fright jellifying his arms.

And something in there, something unseen but mumbling,
grabs both the ball and his wrists.
Something clammy and damp.
It won't let go no matter how hard he tugs and jerks.
And it seems to want to yank him into this dark, musty world
where darkness and stuffiness are ever present;
from where there is no escape,
from where no light emerges,
and where terror grows in its birth-nest.

John Rice

# Spider!

The spider's glued to the ceiling
like a black boil, a bad grudge,
an evil eye.

It's stuck there
like an acid bomb, a black blot,
a vicious blob of grot.

It's waiting its moment,
weighing up its chances.
I can't take my eyes off it!

I can't go to bed for it
in case it comes scurrying, scurrying
on its bristly skittery legs,

bungee-jumping down at me
with its snickety-snackety,
slobbery jaws!

Matt Simpson

# Since that Thunderstorm . . .

Things have been behaving oddly
Ever since that thunderstorm.
It started when the bath plug
Turned transparent, rose
Like a jellyfish in the water,
Tendrils tickling at my toes.
Then there was the telephone
Nibbling my ear, murmuring
'Oh, please . . . Don't put me down.'
The computer mouse began to twitch,
Grew furry in my hand and then ran
Up my arm and disappeared.
I've itched all over ever since.
I tell you, I'm scared. I don't dare
Wear my personal stereo headset.
Well, would you? Just wait.
It hasn't reached you – yet.

Trevor Millum

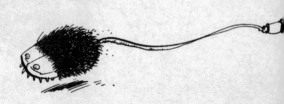

# The Werewolf's Howl

There's a hideous,
horrible,
harrowing howl
and you know that a werewolf's
out on the prowl.
Stoke up the fire,
draw curtains tight,
lock all the doors
and keep out the night.
Don't give the werewolf
a chance to get in
for he's thirsty for blood
and hungry for skin.

The werewolf's a man
with fingernail claws,
hairs on his hands
and slavering jaws.
In anguish and pain
he rages and roars.
He's a werewolf at large in the dark,
in the dark.

The werewolf's a man
with red bloodshot eyes
who bays at the moon
in thunderclap skies.
His sharply fanged teeth
can deeply incise.
He's a werewolf at large in the dark,
in the dark.
The werewolf's a man
who's seeking a feast,
and only warm flesh
will appease the wild beast.
Those caught in his grip
all end up deceased.
He's a werewolf at large in the dark,
in the dark.

There's a hideous,
horrible,
harrowing howl
and you know that a werewolf's
out on the prowl.
Stoke up the fire,
draw curtains tight,
lock all the doors
and keep out the night.
Don't give the werewolf
a chance to get in
for he's thirsty for blood
and hungry for skin.

**Wes Magee**

# The Curse of the Poem on Page 53

It is said
That if you dare read beyond
Line three                                    (Stop reading now!)

And go into the next verse          (Hm. You are brave.)
And into its second line                (Or stupid.)
That something terrible               (That's right – TERRIBLE.)
Will happen to you.                      (Go back while you still can.)

In the third verse                          (Still with us?)
You are warned for the second   (So how many warnings
                                                           do you need?)

And final time                              (And you take no notice.)
Before entering the last verse    (Well go on. I'm not
                                                          stopping you.)

Here you are in the forbidden verse
And you're wondering
What all the fuss was about
You think you are quite safe
But don't look over your shoulder.   (I bet you did.)

John Coldwell

# Desk

It was stuffy in the classroom.
He put his hand inside his desk,
feeling for a pencil. It was cool in there,
he let his hand swing aimlessly around.
The space within seemed vast, and when
he reached in further he found
nothing, could feel no books, no ruler.
His hand floated as if in a bath of shadows,
airy and refreshing, not at all
the same place that the rest of him was in.

He put both hands in, let them drift
deeper, this way and that. It was more than empty,
the inside had no sides. His hands
never reappeared through some unexpected hole.
He lifted the lid quietly a little more. A waft
of soft air cooled his face, the same
as on summer nights or under leafy trees.

He bent his head down to the gap. He looked inside.
Dark as deep water, deep as a clear night sky.
He smiled. He put his head inside.
'What are you doing?' asked the teacher. But he didn't hear.
He slid his shoulders in, and then
before anyone could reach to stop him,
he bent from the waist, kicking his chair back,
and with a muffled cry of pleasure
dived. For a split second,
as the room filled with fresh air,
we watched his legs slide slowly down into the desk
and disappear. And then the lid fell back,
shut, with a soft thud.

**Dave Calder**

# Who's There?

Who's there?
Who's that hiding behind the brown trees,
lurking among the green undergrowth of the woodland?
It's us – the Tree-Elves and the Moss-People
and we are watching you
breaking branches without permission.

Who's there?
Who's that gliding over the wet rocks,
dancing and splashing at the sea's edge?
It's us – the Rock Sirens and Mer-men
and we are watching you
pouring poison in our watery home.

Who's there?
Who's that drifting through the sparkling mist,
flying across bright skies, bursting out of clouds?
It's us – the Alven, we who travel in bubbles of air
and we are watching you
filling our palace of sky with dust and dirt.

Who's there?
Who's that running over the mountains,
wading through cold rivers, striding over forests?
It's us – the Kelpies and Glashans,
the powerful beasts of the wiser world
and we are watching you
wasting these waters and hurting this land.

**John Rice**

# Never Alone at Home

Nessie messes in the bath
There's a dragon in the shed
A yeti's on the settee
A Bigfoot's in my bed.

Gnomes troll in the garden
The kitchen's even worse
Where dear old mummy's pyramid
Has Tutankhamen's Curse.

A vampire's on the ceiling
The wolfman's drinking tea
The poltergeists are very nice
But very scared of me.

My unicorn looks puzzled
When the alien's head is near
Face to face with the thing from space
And its vinyl front ear.

There's a black hole in my bedroom
A time warp near the phone
My house is like a madhouse
I'm never alone at home.

Paul Cookson

# Bigfoot

Our house is full of Bigfoot
or should that be Bigfeet?
We watched them from our window
as they stumbled down the street.

They knocked upon our door
and asked to come inside.
'Don't leave us here,' they pleaded,
'We need a place to hide.'

Now there's Bigfeet in the kitchen
and Biggerfeet in the hall.
On a patch of grass in our garden,
Bigfeet are playing football.

There's Bigfeet in our garage
and Bigfeet in the shed,
while underneath the duvet,
Bigfeet sleep in my bed.

Bigfeet lounge in the lounge
all watching our TV.
There's nowhere much to sit
since they've broken our settee.

Some Bigfoot put his foot
right through our bedroom ceiling.
The darkness in our loft, he said,
was really quite appealing.

The airing cupboard Bigfoot
keeps our water hot.
'No problem at all,' he says,
'I like this job a lot.'

They make an awful racket
up and down our stairs,
they queue to use the bathroom
and block the sink with hairs.

At night they growl and snore,
loud as a thunderstorm,
but all these fur coats everywhere
keep us cosy and warm!

**Brian Moses**

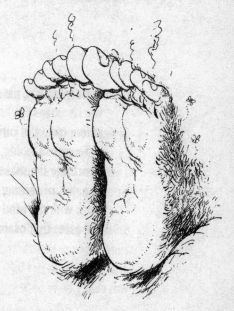

# Gates

Silently, swiftly, pass this place
where moans like breath of death escape,
where creaks of corkscrewed bones, and cracks
of fingers snapping, talloned taps,
punctuate the shake of chains
as hands of seeking, searching veins
work with the wind to wrestle free
the gates that guard the
                                        cemetery.

**Gina Douthwaite**

# BEWARE OF THE GHO*T

There'* a gho*t in my hou*e
Quiet a* mou*e
*teal the letter *
Leave* my life a me**

Take* the letter*
From the *ugar and the *oap
Replaces them with *tar *
I don't think I can cope!

There'* a gho*t in my room
Leaving *tar* around
*inging *ong* of gloom
With a *tarry ***y *ound.

I need my ** back!
I need to *ing my *ong*!
Put the *tar* right back
In the *ky where they belong!

There'* a gho*t in my hou*e
Quiet a* a mou*e
*teal* the letter *
Leave* my life a me**

Ian McMillan

# A selected list of poetry books available from Macmillan

The prices shown below are correct at the time of going to press. However, Macmillan Publishers reserve the right to show new retail prices on covers which may differ from those previously advertised.

---

### Who Rules the School?
Poems chosen by Paul Cookson

0 330 35199 0
£2.99

### Teachers' Pets
Poems chosen by Paul Cookson

0 330 36868 0
£2.99

### Ridiculous Relatives
Poems chosen by Paul Cookson

0 330 37105 3
£2.99

### Tongue Twisters and Tonsil Twizzlers
Poems chosen by Paul Cookson

0 330 34941 4
£2.99

### The Secret Lives of Teachers
Revealing rhymes, chosen by Brian Moses

0 330 34265 7
£3.50

### 'Ere we Go!
Football poems, chosen by David Orme

0 330 32986 3
£2.99

### Parent-Free Zone
Poems about parents, chosen by Brian Moses

0 330 34554 0
£2.99

---

All Macmillan titles can be ordered at your local bookshop
or are available by post from:

**Book Service by Post**
PO Box 29, Douglas, Isle of Man IM99 1BQ

Credit cards accepted. For details:
Telephone: 01624 675137  Fax: 01624 670923
E-mail: bookshop@enterprise.net

**Free postage and packing in the UK.**
Overseas customers: add £1 per book (paperback)
and £3 per book (hardback).